The I AM!
Affirmation Book

Discovering the Value of Who You Are

I0134414

by Steve Viglione

Illustrated by Becky Parish
Graphic Design by Terri Wright
Translated by Marilyn Stompler and
Interpreters UnlimitedTM

English-French Edition

Published by The I AM Foundation
www.iamfoundation.org

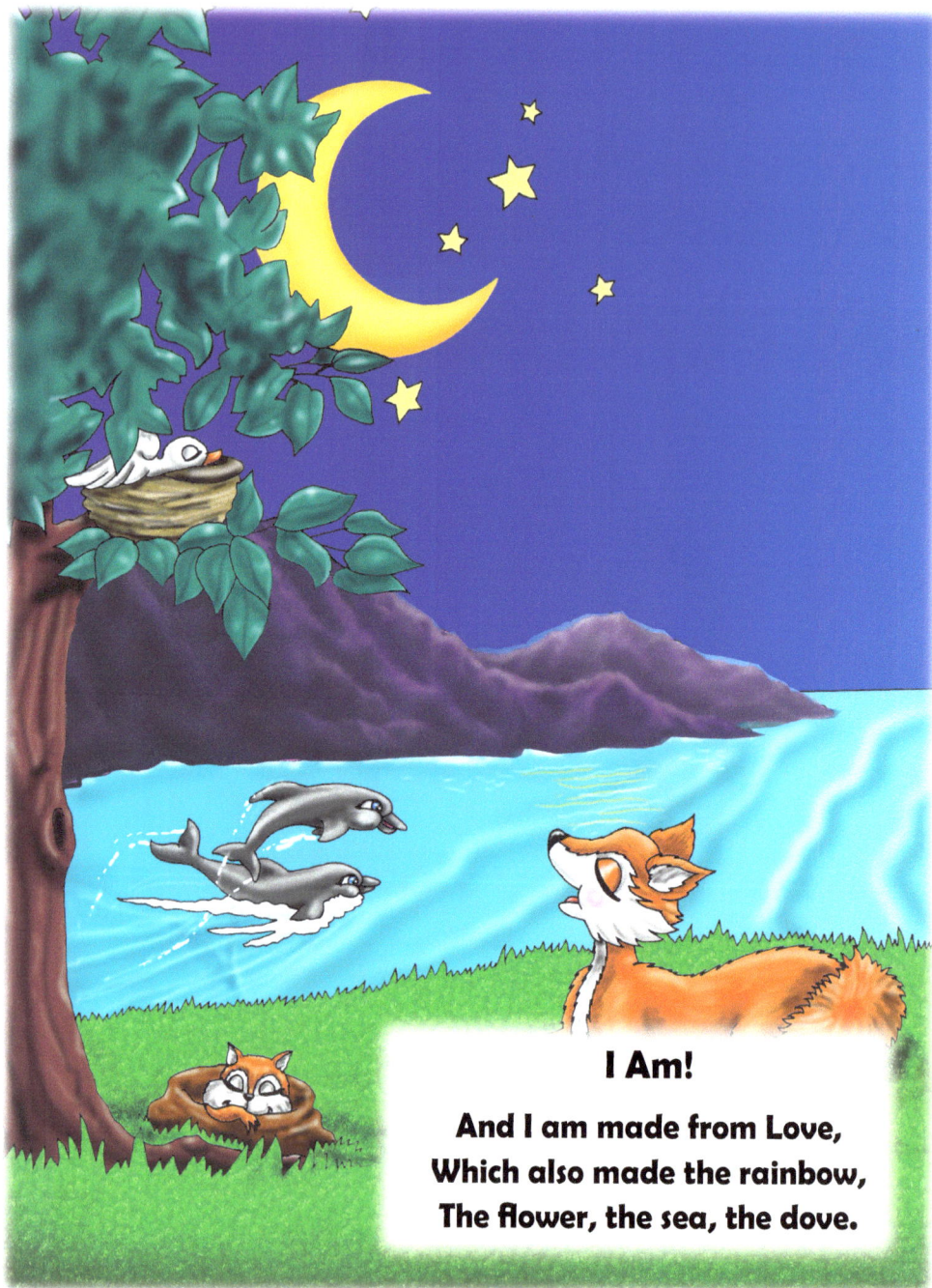

I Am!

And I am made from Love,
Which also made the rainbow,
The flower, the sea, the dove.

Je Suis!
Et j'ai été conçu dans l'Amour,
Qui a aussi fait l'arc-en-ciel,
La fleur, la mer, la colombe.

I Am!

And with everything I am One,
The plants, the trees, the animals,
The stars, the moon, the sun.

Je Suis!
Et avec le monde je ne forme qu'un,
Les plantes, les arbres, les animaux,
Les étoiles, la lune, le soleil.

3

I Am Priceless!

There's nothing worth more than me,
Whether it's the whole world,
Or the smallest thing you can see.

Je N'ai Pas De Prix!

Et rien n'a plus de valeur que moi,
Que ce soit le monde entier,
Ou la plus petite chose visible.

I Am Greatness!

I know others are Greatness too.
If you ask me about yourself,
I will tell you, so are you.

Je Suis Grandeur!
Et je sais que les autres aussi sont grands,
Si tu me demandes ce que je pense de toi,
Je te dirai que toi aussi, tu es grand.

I Am Infinite!

Inside me there is a treasure,
Of gifts I can give to everyone,
Too countless to even measure.

Je Suis Infini!
A l'intérieur de moi il y a un trésor,
De cadeaux que je peux donner à tous,
Trop nombreux pour être comptés.

I Am Worthy!

So there is nothing here on earth,
That can keep me from my Good,
Or take away my worth.

Je Suis Digne d'Estime!
Il n'y a donc rien ici sur terre,
Qui puisse me retenir de ma Bonté,
Ou m'ôter ma dignité.

I Am Joy!

And everywhere I go,
People have to stop,
To appreciate my glow.

Je Suis Joie!
Et partout où je vais,
Les gens doivent s'arrêter,
Pour admirer comme je rayonne!

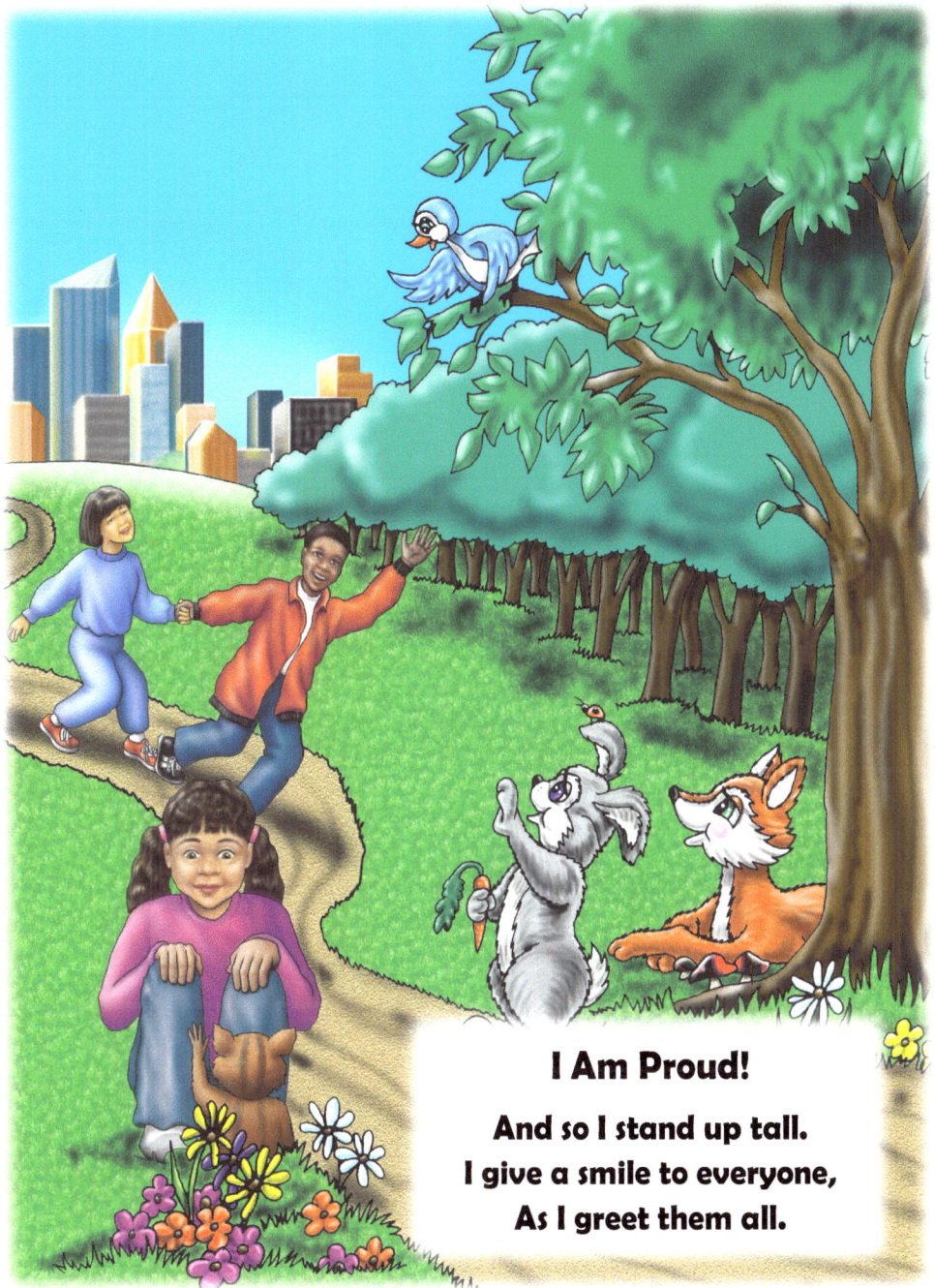

I Am Proud!

And so I stand up tall.
I give a smile to everyone,
As I greet them all.

Je Suis Fierté!
Et de ce fait je me tiens tout droit.
J'offre un sourire à tous,
Lorsque je les salue.

9

I Am Powerful!

Because of the Greatness that's in me,
It's the truth of who I am,
The truth I am to be.

Je Suis Puissance!
A cause de la Grandeur qu'il y a en moi,
C'est le veritable moi,
Celui que je dois être.

I Am Strong!

And I know how unique I am.
I have what it takes,
To be the Me I am.

Je Suis Force!
Et je sais combien je suis unique.
J'ai ce qu'il faut,
Pour être le Moi que je suis.

I Am Vision!

Seeing the Plan that's in store for me,
I listen when I'm quiet,
To my heart which holds the key.

Je Suis Vision!
Voyant le Projet que l'on a pour moi,
J'écoute, tranquille,
Mon coeur qui en détient la clé.

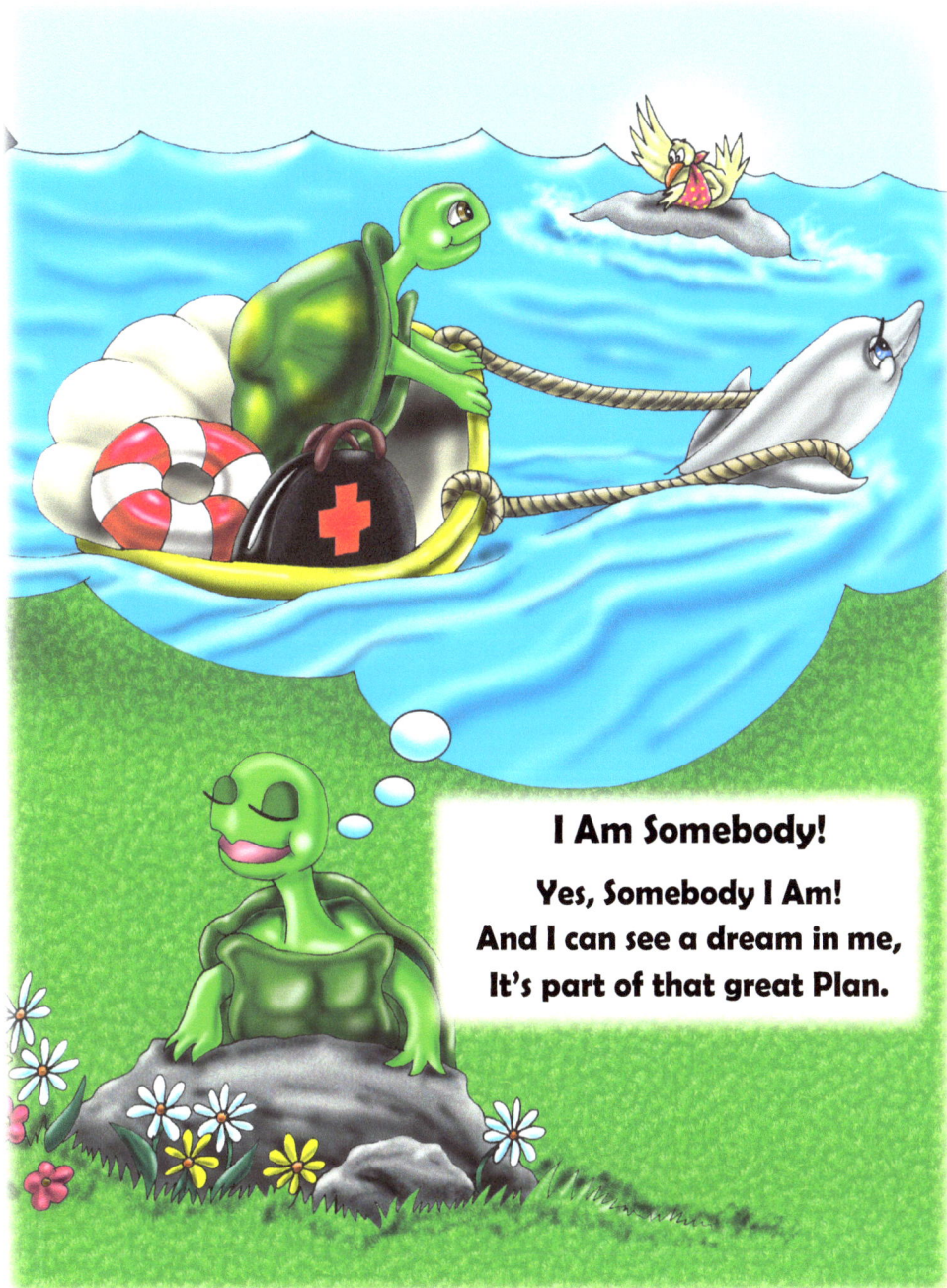

I Am Somebody!

Yes, Somebody I Am!
And I can see a dream in me,
It's part of that great Plan.

Je Suis Quelqu'un!
Oui, je suis vraiment quelqu'un!
Et je peux voir un rêve en moi,
Qui fait partie de ce grand Projet.

I Am Confidence!

Regardless of what others say or do,
I simply believe in myself,
And the Dream I've set my mind to.

Je Suis Confiance!
Malgre ce que disent ou font les autres,
Je crois simplement en moi,
Et en ce Rêve que je me suis fixé.

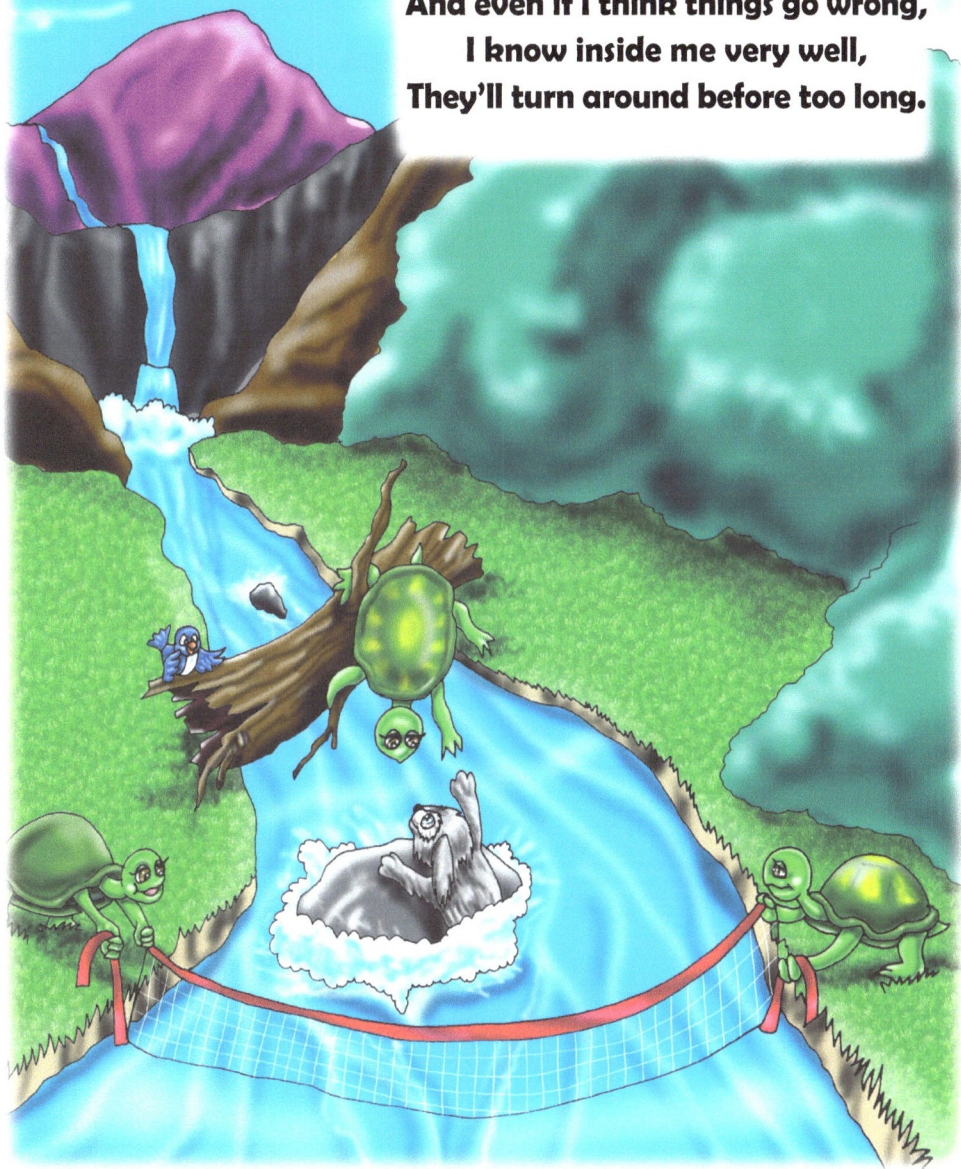

I Am Patience!

And even if I think things go wrong,
I know inside me very well,
They'll turn around before too long.

Je Suis Patience!
Et même si je pense que les choses vont mal,
Je sais bien au plus profond de moi-même,
Que tout s'arrangera très vite.

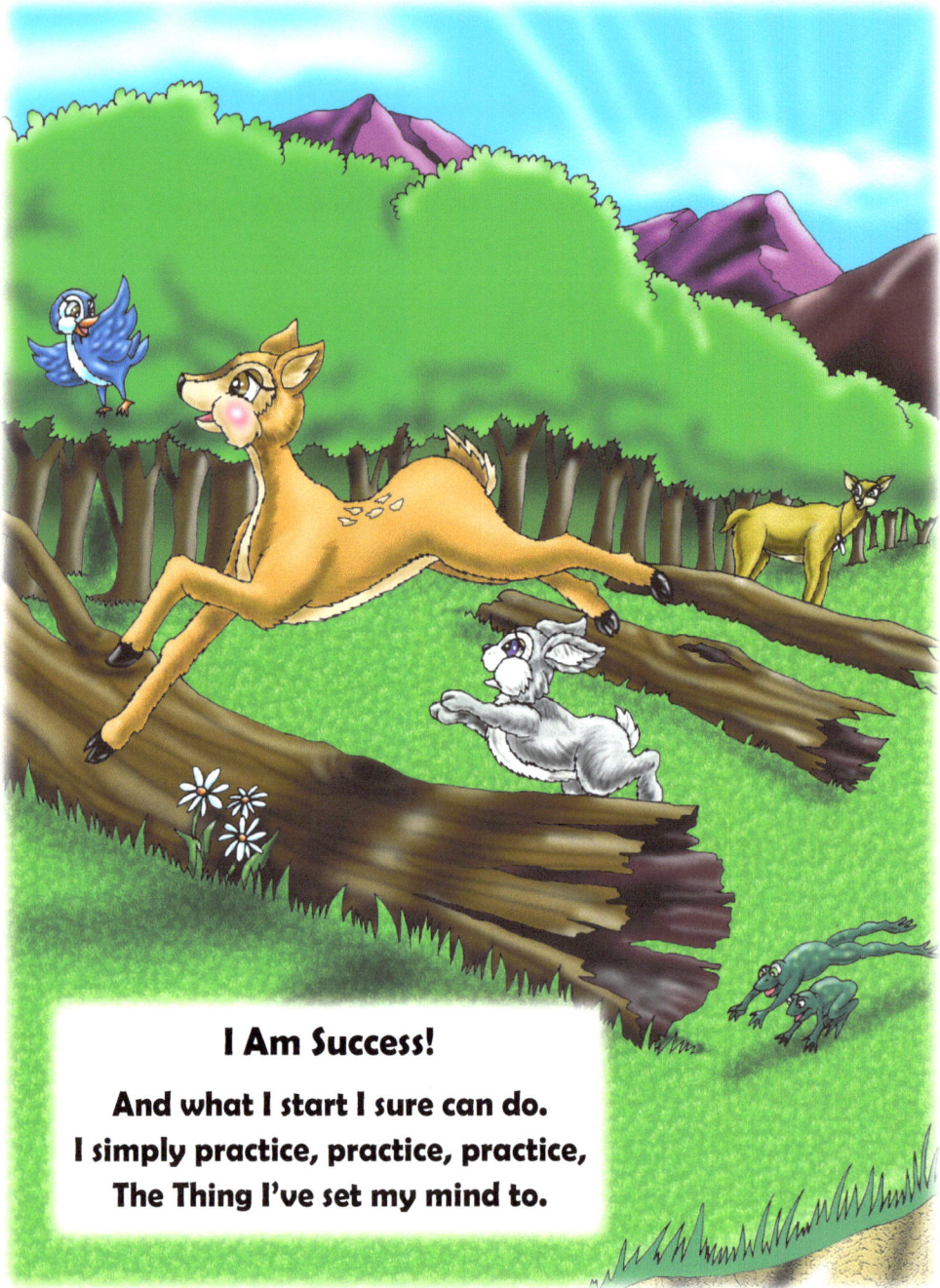

I Am Success!

And what I start I sure can do.
I simply practice, practice, practice,
The Thing I've set my mind to.

Je Suis Succès!
Et ce que je commence, je peux le terminer.
Je m'entraîne, m'entraîne, m'entraîne toujours et encore,
Pour atteindre mon Objectif.

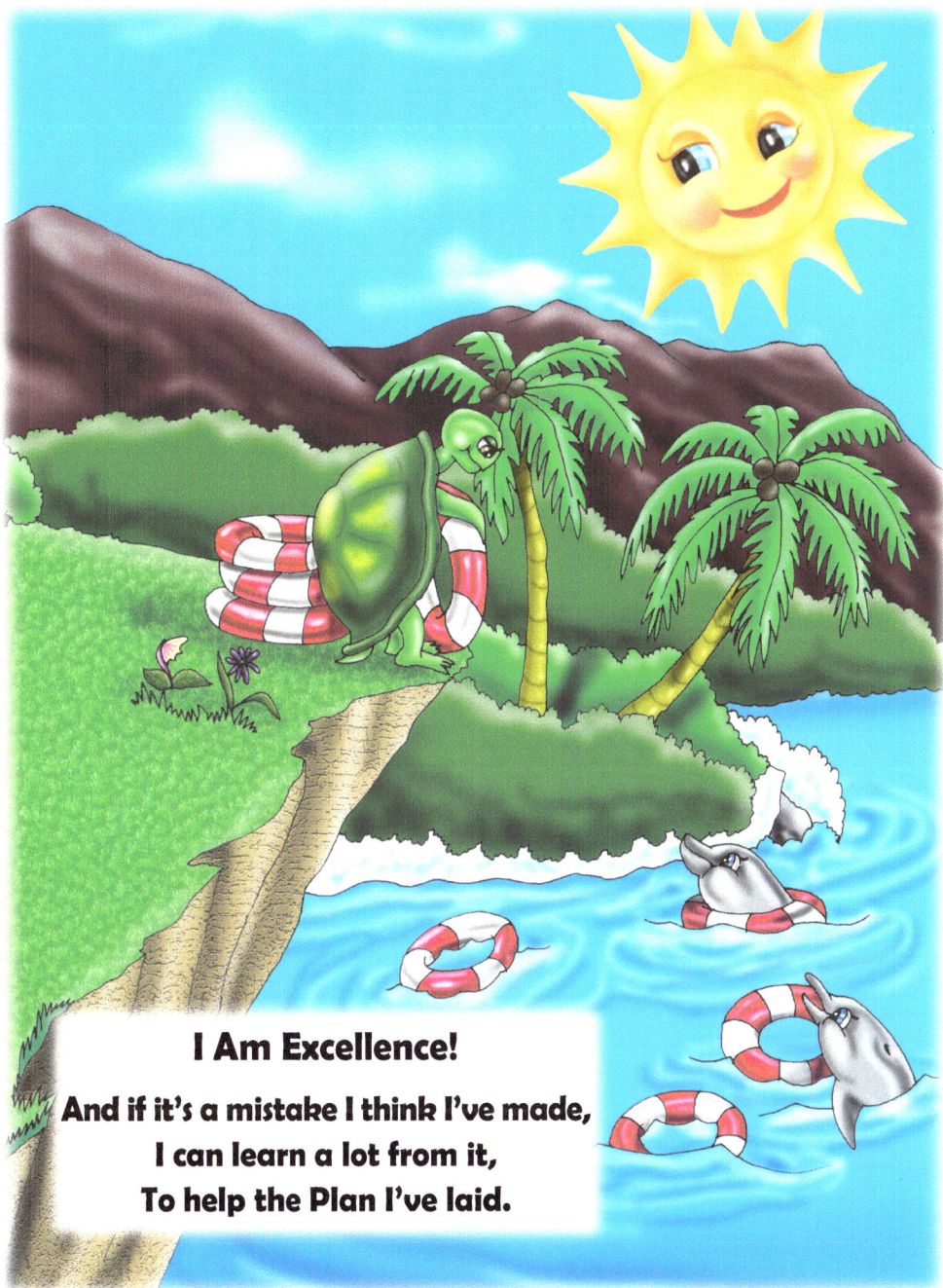

I Am Excellence!

And if it's a mistake I think I've made,
I can learn a lot from it,
To help the Plan I've laid.

Je Suis Excellence!
Et si je pense avoir commis une erreur,
Je m'en sers pour apprendre,
Et faire avancer mon Projet.

I Am Wholeness!

And I Love the body that I'm in.
I accept myself and others.
When I come from Love I win.

Je Suis Santé!
Et j'Aime le corps dans lequel je suis.
Je m'accepte et j'accepte les autres.
Lorsque je suis plein d'Amour je gagne.

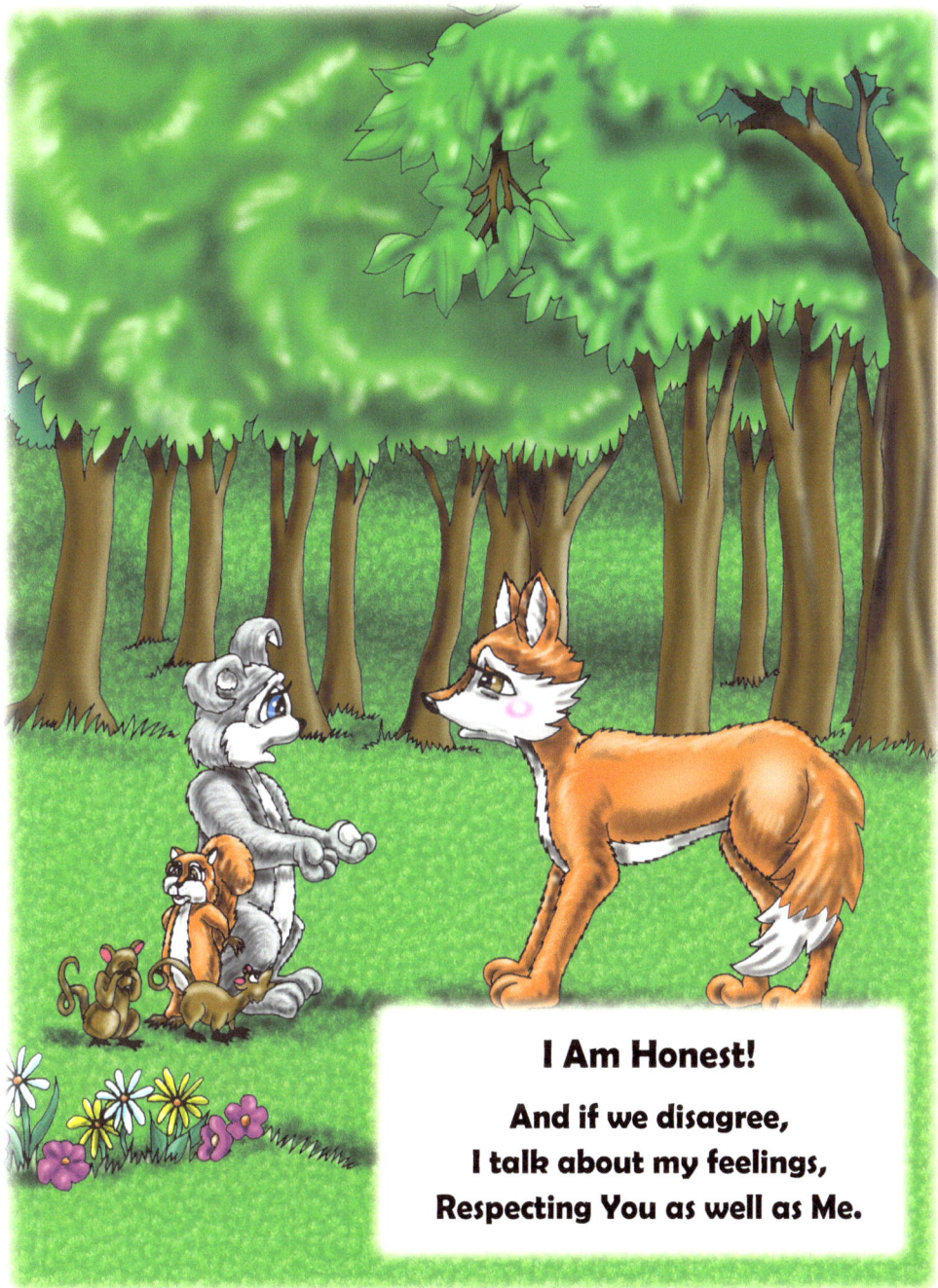

I Am Honest!

And if we disagree,
I talk about my feelings,
Respecting You as well as Me.

Je Suis Honnête!
Et si nous ne sommes pas d'accord,
Je parle de mes sentiments,
En Te respectant aussi bien que Moi.

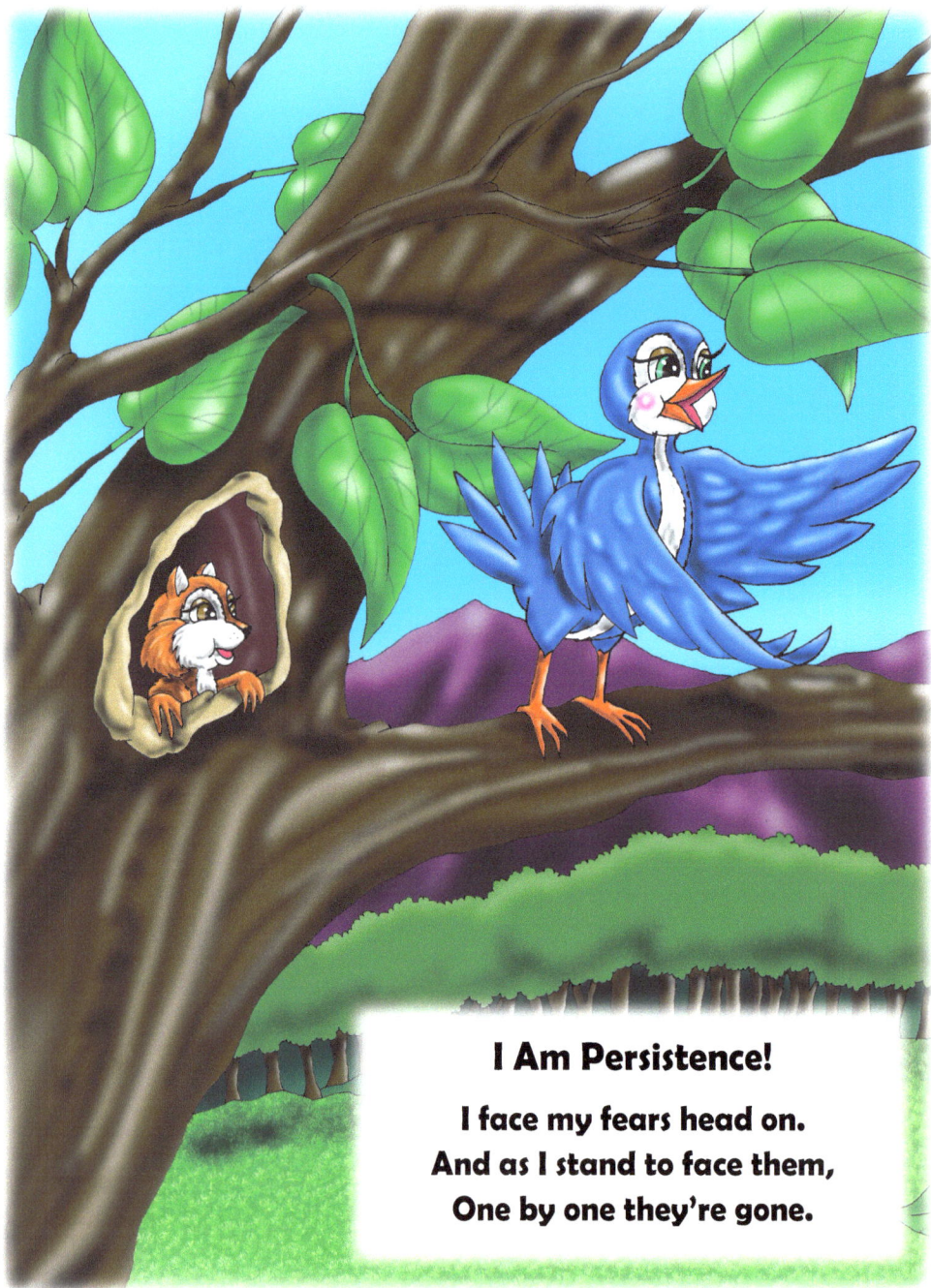

I Am Persistence!

I face my fears head on.
And as I stand to face them,
One by one they're gone.

Je Suis Persistence!
J'affronte mes peurs la tête haute.
Et lorsque je m'arrête pour leur faire face,
Une à une elles disparaissent.

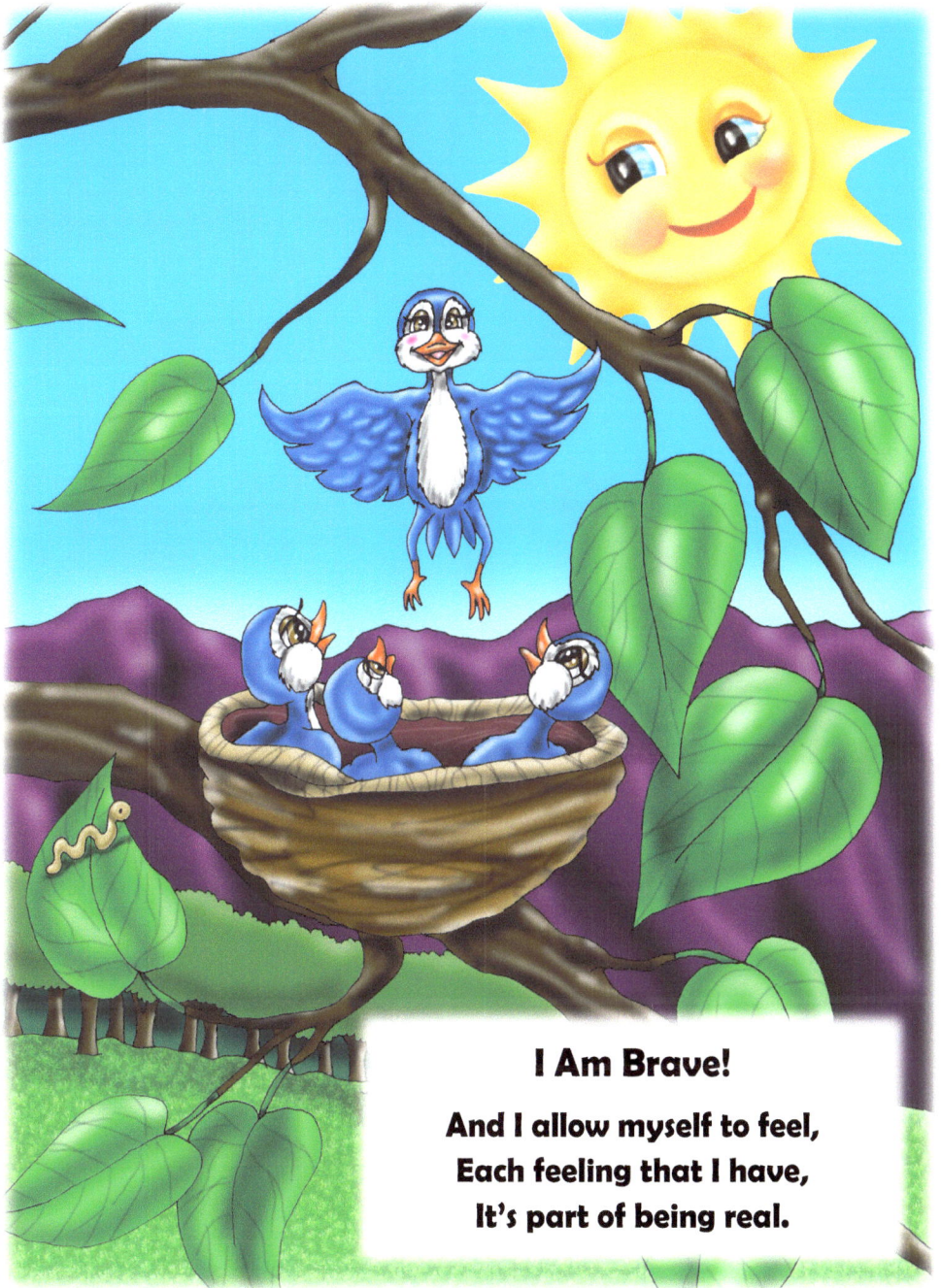

I Am Brave!

And I allow myself to feel,
Each feeling that I have,
It's part of being real.

Je Suis Courageux!
Et je me permets de ressentir,
Chaque sentiment que j'ai,
Cela fait partie d'être réel.

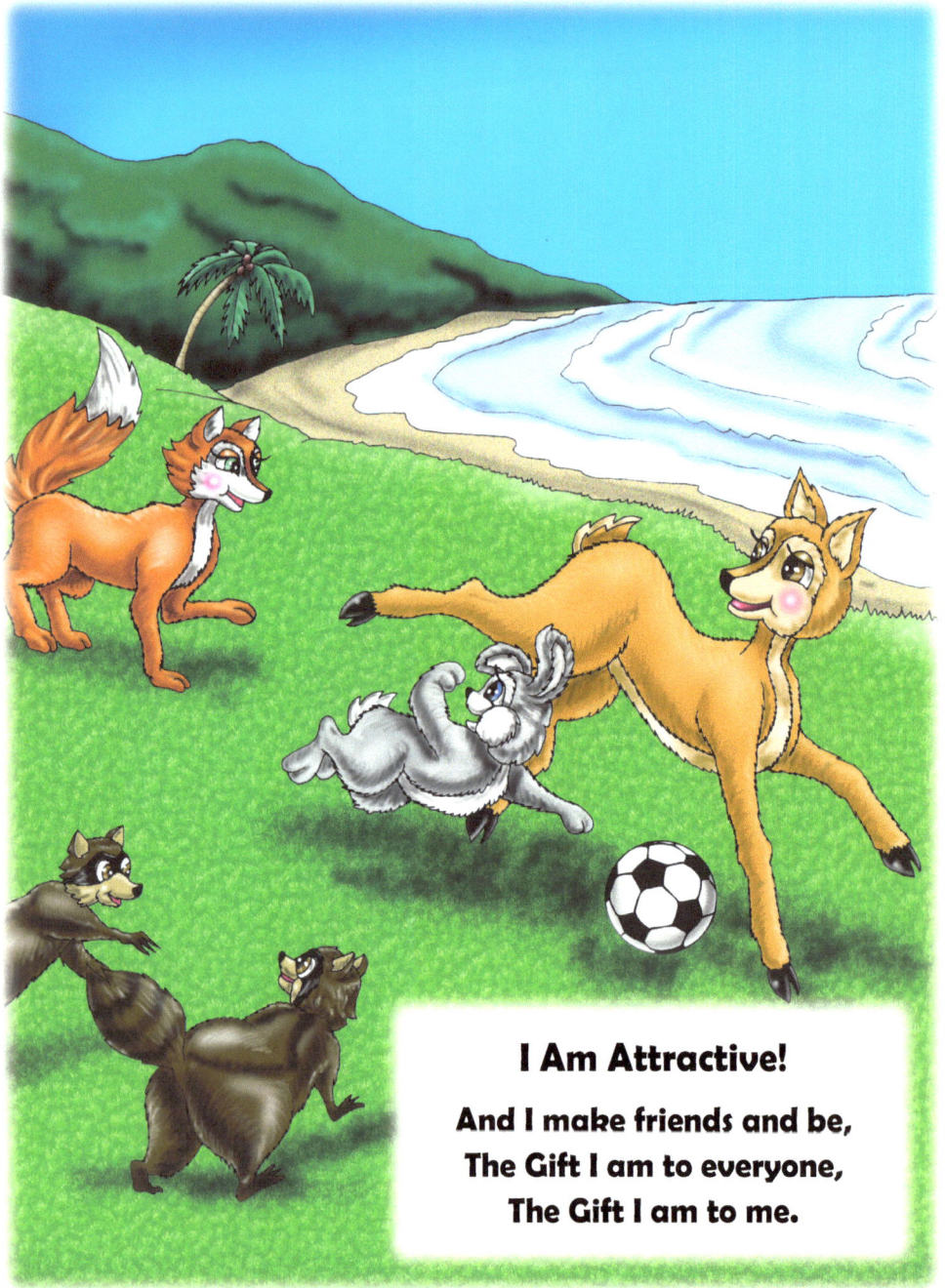

I Am Attractive!

And I make friends and be,
The Gift I am to everyone,
The Gift I am to me.

Je Suis Seduisant!
Et je me fais des amis et je suis,
Le Cadeau pour chacun,
Le Cadeau pour moi-même.

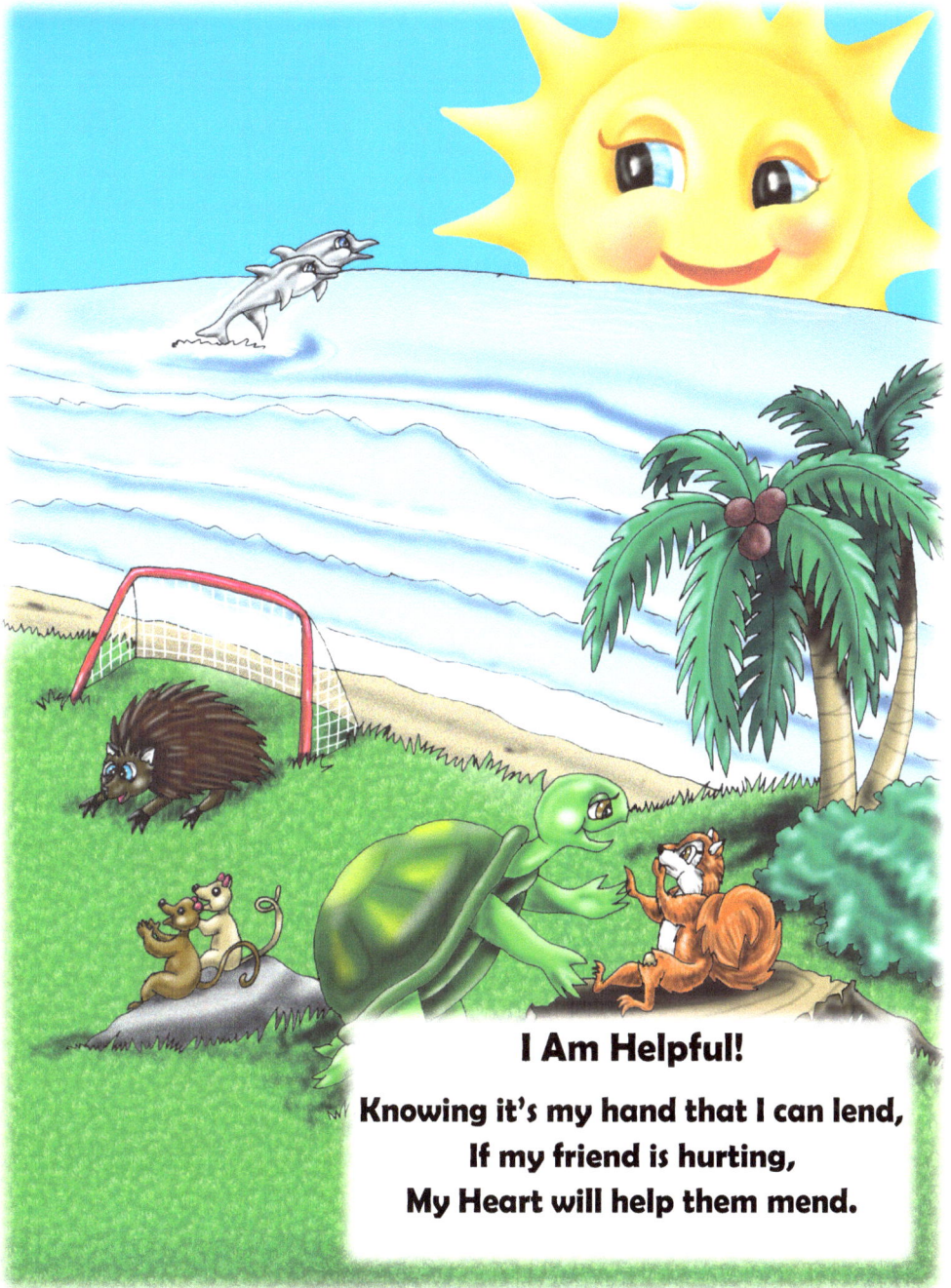

I Am Helpful!

Knowing it's my hand that I can lend,
If my friend is hurting,
My Heart will help them mend.

Je Suis Serviable!
Je sais apporter mon soutien,
Si mon ami souffre,
Mon Coeur l'aidera à guérir.

23

I Am Brilliance!

**And of all the things I know,
Helping one another is the
Greatest way to grow.**

**Je Suis Brilliance!
Et de toutes les choses que je connaisse,
S'entraider est
Le meilleur moyen pour grandir.**

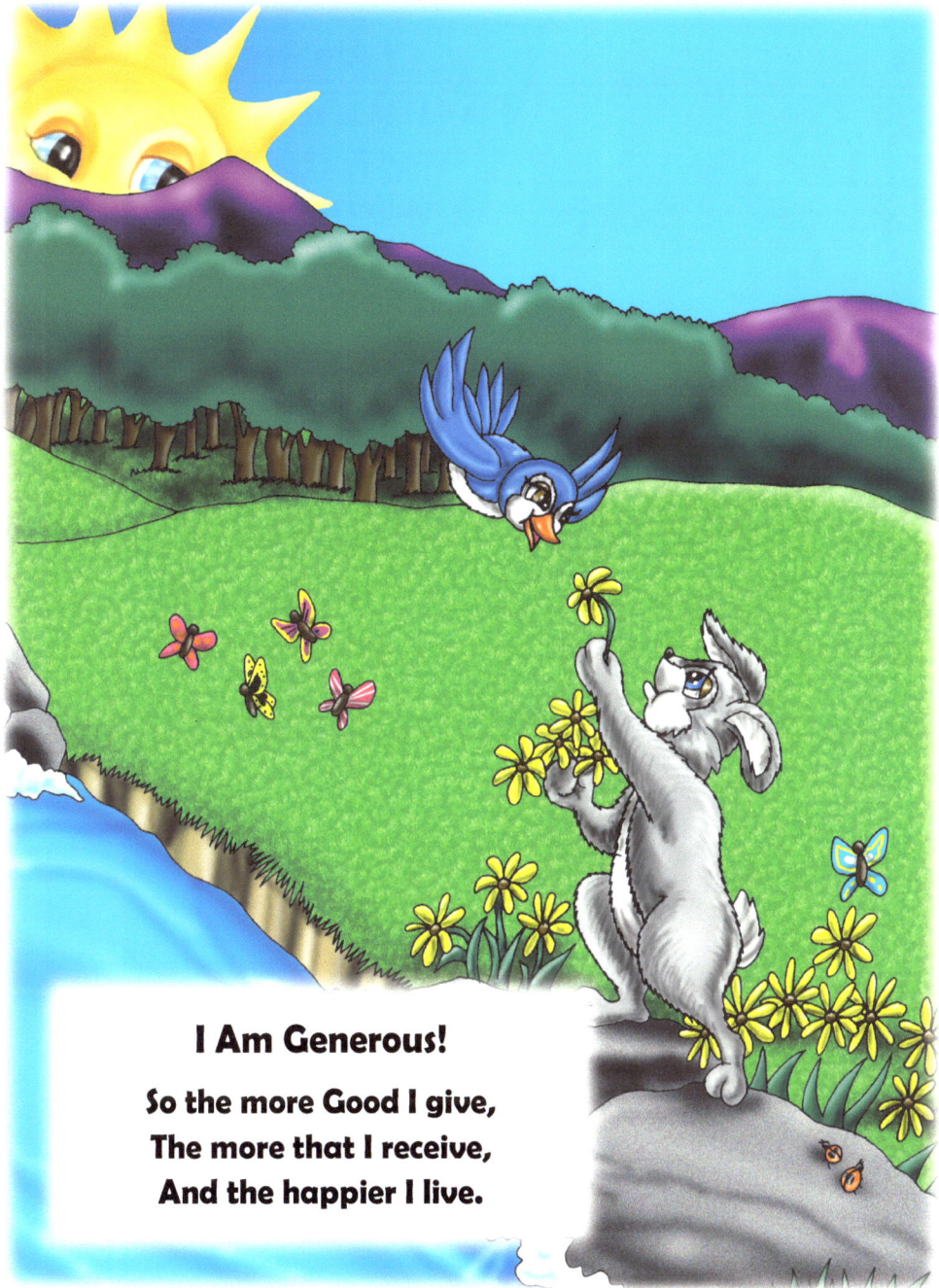

I Am Generous!

So the more Good I give,
The more that I receive,
And the happier I live.

Je Suis Généreux!
Plus je donne,
Plus je reçois,
Et plus je vis heureux.

I Am Peaceful!

And I love the grass so green.
When I'm lying down in it,
It makes me King or Queen.

Je Suis Paisible!
Et j'aime l'herbe si verte,
Quand je me couche dessus,
Cela fait de moi un Roi ou une Reine.

I Am Freedom!

And on a breezy summer night,
I love to see the stars,
The moon, its shape, its light.

Je Suis Liberté!
Et une nuit d'été avec de la brise,
J'aime regarder les étoiles,
La lune, sa forme, sa lumière.

I Am Abundance!

And in Nature I am rich,
I count its many blessings,
There's one in every niche.

Je Suis Abondance!
Et grâce à la Nature je suis riche,
Je compte ses nombreuses benedictions,
Il y en a une dans chaque coin.

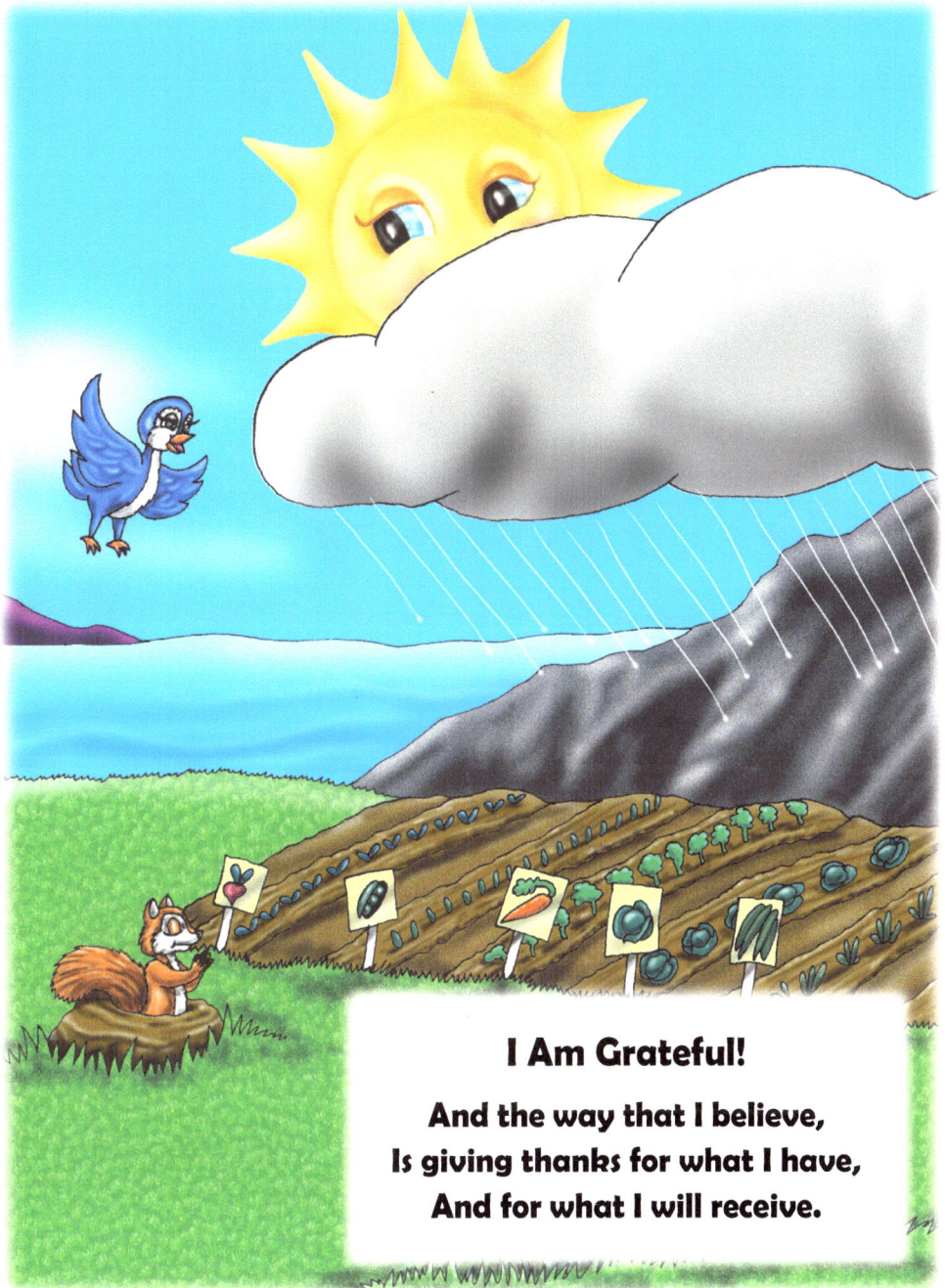

I Am Grateful!

**And the way that I believe,
Is giving thanks for what I have,
And for what I will receive.**

Je Suis Reconnaissant!
Et la chose à laquelle je crois,
C'est de remercier pour ce que j'ai,
Et pour ce que je recevrai.

29

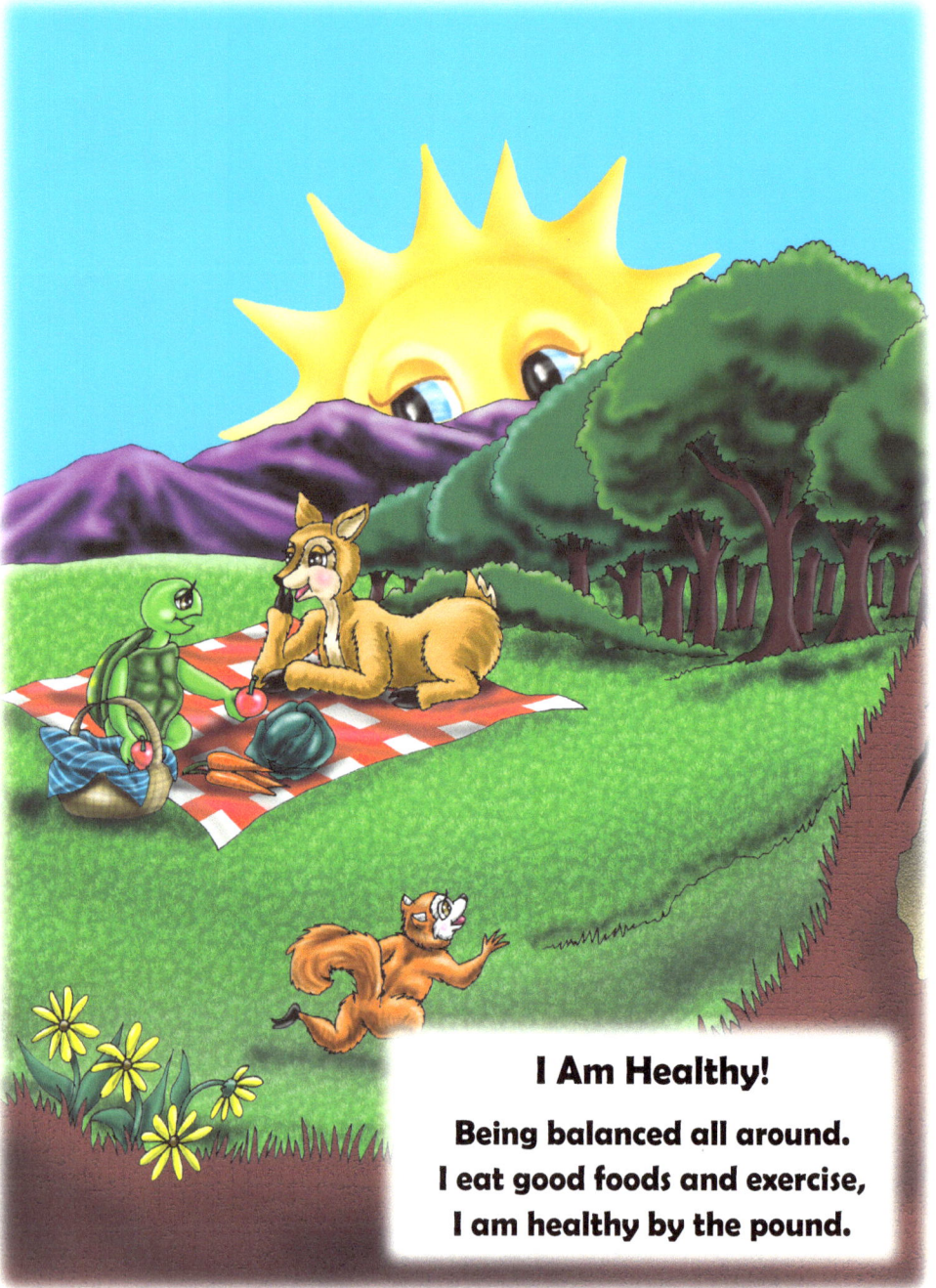

I Am Healthy!

**Being balanced all around.
I eat good foods and exercise,
I am healthy by the pound.**

**Je Suis Sain!
Parfaitement équilibré.
Je me nourris bien et je fais du sport,
Je suis en bonne santé et de bon poids.**

I Am Wisdom!

Thinking Good with every thought,
Being guided from within,
My direction is self-taught.

Je Suis Sagesse!
En pensant du Bien à chaque pensée,
Etant guidé de l'intérieur,
Je m'oriente tout seul.

I Am Loving!

In each and every way.
In fact it's what I tell myself
At the start of each new day.

Je Suis Aimant!
Toute manière et tout le temps.
En fait c'est ce que je me dis
Au début de chaque nouvelle journée.

Now I know who I Am,

And when I close my eyes I see,
The incredible child that I am,
The I Am, that is Me.

Maintenant Je sais qui Je Suis,
Et quand je ferme mes yeux je vois,
L'enfant incroyable que je suis,
Le vrai Moi, l'Etre que je suis.

A Note from the Author

The I AM! Affirmation Book: Discovering the Value of Who You Are was inspired by my children, Alexia and Tyler. I wrote it because I had a deep desire to do something for their generation and to help make the world a little brighter and better. Whatever age you are, the book is meant to be a gift for this incredible person called you. Wherever you are, how tall or short you think you may be, how much you weigh or what you look like; Your value exists within you and not in what the world may or may not tell you.

How do I know this? I know this because I lived it. I grew up with low self-esteem and suffered inside because I put my value in things outside myself. When I discovered that my value comes from within, my self-esteem greatly improved. It is my hope and intention that somehow and in some way **The I AM! Affirmation Book: Discovering the Value of Who You Are** makes an incredible difference in your life.

- Steve Viglione, Author and Founder of The I AM Foundation

Une Note de L'auteur

Le livre d'affirmation **Je SUIS! Découvrir la Valeur de Qui Tu Es** m'a été inspiré par mes enfants, Alexia et Tyler. J'ai écrit ce livre car j'avais un désir profond de faire quelque chose pour leur génération et d'aider à rendre le monde meilleur et plus brillant. Quelque soit ton âge, ce livre se veut un cadeau pour l'être incroyable que tu es. Peu importe ce que le monde te dit, ou que tu sois, quels que soient ta taille, ton poids ou ton physique, tu as de la valeur!

Comment puis-je le savoir? Je le sais car je l'ai vécu. J'ai grandi avec peu d'estime de moi-même et j'ai souffert car je plaçais ma valeur dans les choses extérieures. Quand j'ai découvert que ma valeur venait de l'intérieur, mon estime s'est nettement améliorée. J'ai l'espoir que, d'une certaine façon, le livre **Je SUIS! Découvrir la Valeur de Qui Tu Es** fasse une différence incroyable dans ta vie.

- Steve Viglione, Auteur et Fondateur de la Foundation I AM

A Note from the Vice President of The I AM Foundation

The I AM! Affirmation Book: Discovering the Value of Who You Are is dedicated to the children of the world, who are our future hope for peace. When children discover their value, they bring value to their family, their nation and the world. The children are depending on us and we are depending on them.

- Marilyn Powers, Ph.D.

Une note du vice-président Le JE SUIS de la Fondation

Le livre Je SUIS! Découvrir la Valeur de Qui Tu Es est dédié aux enfants du monde, futurs gardiens de notre espoir de paix. Quand les enfants découvrent leur valeur, ils apportent cette valeur à leur famille, leur nation et au monde. Les enfants comptent sur nous et nous comptons sur eux.

- Dra. Marilyn Powers

Dr. Marilyn Powers and Steve Viglione of The I AM Foundation. Marilyn and Steve are happily married and live in California.

Docteur Marilyn Powers et Steve Viglione de la I AM Foundation. Marilyn et Steve forment un couple heureux et vivent en Californie.

The I AM Foundation's
Buy-One, Gift-One Program
"Whenever you purchase a Love~Wisdom Series™ book,
another book is gifted to a child somewhere in the world."

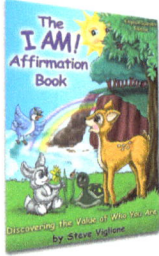

The I AM! Affirmation Book and Curriculum
Discovering the Value of
Who You Are
By Steve Viglione
For pre-K through 4th grade

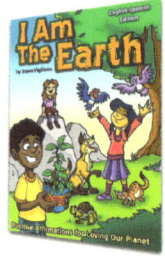

I Am The Earth and Curriculum
Positive Affirmations
for Loving Our Planet
By Steve Viglione
For pre-K through 6th grade

The I AM! Affirmation Book For Teens and Young Adults
Empowering Who You Are
By Steve Viglione

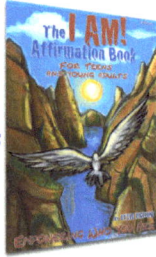

I Am Healthy!
Affirmations for
Health and Well-Being
By Steve Viglione
For pre-K through 6th grade

Words of Power
Affirmations for Loving
your Age, Work & Life
By Dr. Marilyn Powers
An empowering guide
for adults

The Bridge and Companion Workbook
A Seven-Stage Map to
Redefine Your Life
and Purpose
By Dr. Marilyn Powers
For adults moving through
change and transition

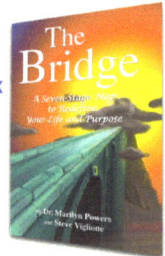

Make a profound impact by
ordering books or making a donation to support our programs at
http://www.iamfoundation.org
or call 619.297.7010

Follow Us On:

LOVE WISDOM Series™

About The I AM Foundation

The I AM Foundation is a 501(c)(3) educational non-profit organization whose mission is empowering children and adults, worldwide, through publishing and gifting The Love~Wisdom Series. The organization was founded in 1998, and since then has gifted and distributed over one million books and products, worldwide.

Our signature book, *The I AM! Affirmation Book: Discovering The Value of Who You Are* is being translated into 50 different languages and has been gifted in over 50 countries and counting. *I Am The Earth: Positive Affirmations for Loving Our Planet* was published for the 40th Anniversary of Earth Day in 2010 and was featured during Earth Day week on the PR Newswire Billboard in Times Square in New York City. *Words of Power: Affirmations for Loving Your Age, Work, and Life* and *The Bridge: A Seven-Stage Map to Redefine Your Life and Purpose* are books that empower adults and entire communities to make dynamic change and move them forward in positive, new directions. There are now ten published titles in The Love~Wisdom Series for children and adults.

If you feel inspired by the work of The I AM Foundation, you can join us in positively impacting children and adults across the globe by gifting books from *The Love~Wisdom Series*.

Please visit www.iamfoundation.org, or call 619.297.7010, to learn more about The I AM Foundation. You may wish to:

• Volunteer, make a tax-deductible donation, sponsor, purchase, or apply to receive books from our program.
• Invite authors and Co-Founders Steve Viglione and Dr. Marilyn Powers to speak at your company, school, or organization.
• Sign up to receive our newsletter. We'd love to add you to our list.